Prison Planet

How to Avoid Becoming Another Statistic

How to Avoid Becoming Another Statistic

Brandon McClain J.D.

For information contact:

info@uptownmediaventures.com

Book and Cover design by Team Uptown

First Edition: December 2020

ISBN: 978-1-68121-127-5

10 9 8 7 6 5 4 3 2 1

Dedicated to any and all people who have no desire to become another statistic.

DISCLAIMER

Nothing in this book is represented to be or should be considered legal advice. The reader should always consult with their own attorney for such.

Table of Contents

Introduction

According to the Institute for Criminal Policy Research (ICPR) on its 2018 World Prison Population list, over 11 million people are imprisoned in the world. Some should be due to heinous offenses. Others are imprisoned because of non-violent crimes, while others have been imprisoned for being activists for social change. Many are imprisoned because of lack of funding to pay for a bail to get them out.

The reasons run the gamut, but the fact remains that in many countries, like the United States, prisons have become profit centers and there is a push to increase the numbers who are imprisoned. Thus, in a clandestine fashion, with the use of mediums such as movies and rap music, criminality is being promoted. Many of the very companies that promotes such lifestyles, also own stock in some of the largest private prisons in the U.S.

Also, the use of technology by governments and corporations alike serve to influence and even control the thoughts and movement of the masses. Thus, a persona can be technically free, but subject to such a high degree of control, that they could be in a de facto imprisonment.

This book focuses on the prison system of the United States. This is because the United States leads the world in the imprisonment of its citizens.

The issue of mass incarceration remains – how far will the grip of control go? What can and should the masses unite to do about it? In the meantime, we are all dealing with the increasing threat of living in a prison planet.

The United States Prison System

The United States leads the world in many things. It used to lead the world in productivity and education. Now the U.S. leads the world in incarceration with 2.2 million people currently in the nation's prisons and jails — a 500% increase over the last forty years. Changes in sentencing law and policy, not changes in crime rates, explain most of this increase. These trends have resulted in prison overcrowding and fiscal burdens on states to accommodate a rapidly expanding penal system.

According to the Sentencing Project, "A series of law enforcement and sentencing policy changes of the "tough on crime" era resulted in dramatic growth in incarceration. Since the official beginning of the War on Drugs in the 1980s, the number of people incarcerated for drug offenses in the U.S. skyrocketed from 40,900 in 1980 to 452,964 in 2017. Today, there are more people behind bars for a drug offense than the number of people who were in prison or jail for any crime in 1980. The number of people sentenced to prison for property and violent crimes has also increased even during periods when crime rates have declined."

Harsh sentencing laws like mandatory minimums, combined with cutbacks in parole release, keep people in prison for longer periods of time. The National Research Council reported that half of the 222% growth in the state prison population between 1980 and 2010 was due to an increase of time served in prison for all offenses. There has also been a historic rise in the use of life sentences: one in nine people in prison is now serving a life sentence, nearly a third of whom are sentenced to life without parole.

As of 2018 there are not only 2.3 million inmates, but also 6.7 million people under correctional control, which includes not only incarceration but also probation and parole.

The King of the Draconians

Draco, also called Drako or Drakon, was the first recorded legislator of Athens in Ancient Greece. He replaced the prevailing system of oral law and blood feud by a written code to be enforced only by a court of law. **Draconian** is an adjective **meaning** "of great severity", that derives from Draco, an Athenian law scribe under whom small offenses had heavy punishments (Draconian laws).

According to The Sentencing Project, "The United States is the world's leader in incarceration with 2.2 million people currently in the nation's prisons and jails — a 500% increase over the last forty years. Changes in sentencing law and policy, not changes in crime rates, explain most of this increase."

In the United States, most of the drug offenders are in federal prisons (47.1 %); while the state prisons have over three times less (14.4 %). Most of the violent offenders are in state prisons (55.7 %), while the federal prisons have nearly seven times less (7.8 %).

Brandon McClain

The 2018 International Center for Prison Reform indicates: "There are more than 2.1 million prisoners in the United States of America, 1.65 million in China (plus unknown numbers in pre-trial detention and other forms of detention), 690,000 in Brazil, 583,000 in the Russian Federation, 420,000 in India, 364,000 in Thailand, 249,000 in Indonesia, 233,000 in Turkey, 230,000 in Iran, 204,000 in Mexico and 188,000 in the Philippines.

The countries with the highest prison population rate – that is, the number of prisoners per 100,000 of the national population – are the United States (655 per 100,000), followed by El Salvador (604), Turkmenistan (552), U.S. Virgin Islands (542), Thailand (526), Cuba (510), Maldives (499), Northern Mariana Islands – U.S.A. (482), British Virgin Islands (470), Rwanda (464), Bahamas (438), Seychelles (437), Grenada (435), St Vincent and the Grenadines (426), Guam – U.S.A. (404) and Russian Federation (402)."

For a country of 328.2 million in 2019, the percentage of incarcerated may seem small, involving five grams of crack, as opposed to 500 grams of cocaine, is assigned a five-year minimum sentence.4

This 100 to I ratio is duplicated in the United States Sentencing Guidelines promulgated by the U.S. Sentencing Commission in 1987.42 The distinction made between crack and powder cocaine in the mandatory sentencing provisions of the Anti-Drug Abuse Act and the Sentencing Guidelines has been heavily criticized in the decade since its promulgation. Generally, the criticism is that the more severe penalties for crack have a discriminatory effect on black Americans." That is, because crack offenders receive higher sentences than do powder cocaine offenders, and because the vast majority of crack offenders are black,' black defendants go to prison for longer durations than the predominantly white powder cocaine defendants for offenses

On August 3, 2010, President Obama signed the Fair Sentencing Act of 2010 into law.1 This measure eliminated the five-year mandatory minimum prison sentence that previously adhered under federal law upon a conviction for possession of five grams or more of crack cocaine.2 The Act also increased the amount, in weight, of crack that must be implicated for either a five- or a ten-year mandatory minimum sentence to apply upon conviction of any of several federal drug trafficking crimes.3 The latter provision significantly reduces the disparity between the amount of crack that will trigger these mandatory minimums and the amount of powder cocaine that will produce the same results.

Whereas federal law previously treated one hundred grams of powder cocaine as the equivalent of one gram of crack for sentencing purposes, after the Fair Sentencing Act, the statutory ratio now stands at a mere 18:1.5

Prison for Profit - Cash is King

The Police Drove Me to the ATM

This a personal account of how the judicial systems works. When I was in my youth (early 20s), I was arrested by the police department of a local suburb late at night because I got into a fight a few days before. The municipality already had a bail determination.

After I turned myself in, the police officers told that I could be bailed if I had someone bring $300 up to the police station.

I informed the police that I had the money on my bank card and that they could just take the money off the card. They informed me that they were not authorized to make any transactions on my card.

They informed me that if I wanted to make a transaction, they would drive me up to an ATM machine. I ready agreed.

However, the interesting part is that I would have to remain in hand cuffs while I attempted to remove the card from my wallet. Hand cuffs and all, I adroitly place the card in the ATM and pressed the buttons. When the money came out, I held hold to may card and the currency for dear life!

They drove me back to the police station, counted the money and let me go in the middle of the cold night.

This taught me something. ALWAYS keep some money for bail! This might sound crazy because no one anticipates getting into any trouble. But as it relates to the U.S. justice system in just about any jurisdiction – Cash is King!

The Crazy Bail System

According to the 2017 Brooklyn Law Review, "At any given time in America, approximately 70% of all inmates in state and local jails are pretrial detainees.2 The large majority of these individuals are charged with nonviolent offenses and remain incarcerated after arrest—before even going to trial—simply because they cannot afford to pay the bail required for their release."

This a major problem in the United States create a two-tiered system of justice in the United States, where regardless of factual guilt or innocence, a defendant's ability to assist attorneys in mounting a defense against accusations of criminal conduct and withstand prosecutorial pressures to enter a guilty plea is predominately dependent upon their financial standing.4 Meanwhile, the time spent in pretrial detention exacts not only a steep and long-term toll on an indigent defendant's productivity, family unity, and community wellbeing but also an enormous cost on American taxpayers.5 The policies governing criminal procedure should thus be amended to ensure that poor defendants are afforded the same freedom and mobility enjoyed by those with means, as opposed to our current system which predicates access to justice on the ability to pay an oft arbitrarily set bail amount.

Diversion

Diversion is a program that has been created by the state legislature and signed into law. It identifies crimes and offender characteristics that will enable the defendant to enter the program. Under some diversion systems, defendants are "diverted" to counseling early in the proceedings. In some formats, the defendant doesn't have to enter a guilty or <u>no-contest plea</u> in order to receive diversion. Other systems require that the defendant formally admit guilt but suspend punishment until the defendant has had the opportunity to complete diversion. (The plea isn't formally entered into the court system so it can be erased upon successful completion of the program.)

Defendants typically pay for their diversion programs with a fee to the court, treatment center, or both. The cost can sometimes be more than a fine.

Diversion programs can last from six months to a year or more. These programs emphasize counseling, treatment, and behavior modification over punitive measures. Often, participants must agree to attend classes and vocational training, participate in individual or group therapy or counseling, perform community service work, make restitution to any victim, and pay fines.

When participants successfully complete the program, the case returns once and for all to court and is dismissed. If the case is dismissed, the record of the arrest isn't usually sealed or otherwise destroyed. Defendants may be able take the additional step of seeking to expunge, or seal, the record of the case.

If the defendant doesn't complete diversion or is discharged from the program for failure to adhere to its terms (or for subsequent criminal behavior), the case returns to court. If the defendant previously entered a guilty or no-contest plea, then the judge can impose a sentence. If the defendant failed and the form of diversion didn't require her to previously enter such a plea, then she'll have to enter one, and the case will proceed accordingly.

Expungement

If, God forbid, you ever get convicted of a misdemeanor or a non-violent felony. Many states allow for either expungement or sealing of a criminal record.

Expungement and sealing are two different options that remove records from public view. Expungement erases the record so that it's like it never happened. Sealing means that it is just hidden from most of the public's view, but certain agencies and employers can still see it.

Lack of Knowledge of the Law is No Excuse!

Ignorantia juris non excusat or *ignorantia legis neminem excusat* (Latin for "ignorance of the law excuses not" and "ignorance of law excuses no one"[2] respectively) is a legal principle holding that a person who is unaware of a law may not escape liability for violating that law merely by being unaware of its content.

In criminal law, although ignorance may not clear a defendant of guilt, it can be a consideration in sentencing, particularly where the law is unclear or the defendant sought advice from law enforcement or regulatory officials. For example, if a person was charged with being in possession of gambling devices after they had been advised by customs officials that it was legal to import such devices into a country like Canada. Although the defendant was convicted, the sentence was an absolute discharge.

Tips on Not Becoming Another Statistic

1. **Keep at least $1,000 on a card for bail money**. This may sound crazy because no reasonable person ever expects to get into any legal difficulty. However, life has a way of bringing drama to you even if you're not looking for it.

   For example, let's say you're out with some buddies and a fight breaks out with some goons getting the best of your friend. You just might feel compelled to assist your friend from the altercation. Of course, the police may not always get the situation right and all the parties may end up getting arrested. So, unless you plan on playing cards are your house from now on, you would be wise to ensure that you always have access to bail money.

2. **Don't hang out with crazy friends in public (and sometimes private) places**. In many

jurisdictions in the United States and other countries, a person can be deemed guilty by association.

So, what does this mean? It means that you can be charged with a crime just based on your association with a criminal actor.

Don't forget about those accounts of a young guy hanging out with some fake buddies who rob a convenience store when the hapless guy is sitting in the car. Even though he actually had nothing to do with the crime and had no mental state to commit a crime, he can still be charged, especially if some of his "buddies" decide to throw him under the bus in an attempt to save their own hide!

3. **Strive to obey all traffic laws**. Police love stopping people with real or imagined traffic infractions. This means if you can handle having one drink at a bar (which is legal), but that one drink noticeable affects your driving ability (which is illegal), you might want to not

drink at all at a pub and then get into a car. Some people can handle a drink a two and be fine, while other are significantly affected.

4. **Avoid driving vehicles of people you really don't know very well**. This scenario ties into being careful with who we associate with. For example, don't agree to drive a car for someone you really don't know. What if that person is hiding contraband in the vehicle and the police stop you? The Incriminating implications are obvious.

5. **If you are on probation, you must walk on water**. Once false move and an evil probation officer land you back in jail or prison to serve the remainder of your time. You don't want to even get a jay walking ticket or anything that would alert any probation officer to look closer at you.

6. **Strive to learn how to control your own emotions at all times**. The only thing a person can control in this life are their own actions. So, strive to never be a reactionary person who allows emotionalism to influence their actions to their detriment.

7. **Keep your mouth shut!** Whether you are involved in a traffic stop or something worse, like a police interrogation, NEVER freely talk with law enforcement. I don't care if the "good cop" seems like a nice guy. Simply ask to speak to your attorney and say no more. Remember, whatever you say can and WILL BE USED AGAINST YOU!

8. **Make friends in high places**. Let's keep it real. It's not what you know but who you know that makes the difference much of the time. I know it can be a bother sometimes but get to know the police and politicians in your community. You might get a get out of jail free card, at least for a traffic stop anyway.

These connections can be the difference between whether you get charged by the prosecutor's office, a judge locks you up, gives you probation, or even lets you go.

9. **Maintain a legitimate appearance**. It may be wrong or right, but people are judged by their outward appearance. To believe otherwise would be naïve. Nowadays, tattoos are more readily accepted – to a certain degree. But other things such as face tattoos, face piercings, and certain advant garde hair styles may detract from you as a person. This is especially when a person in law enforcement does not know you personally.

    Yes, it's your right to do with your body as you like, but it might be wise to err on the side of caution.

10. **Retain a good attorney**. Nowadays, just because a person is allowed to practice a profession – whether it be in medicine,

accounting, law or any other profession, it's best to do your homework so that you can be sure to have the right representation in a legal situation.

Check out an attorney's online ratings if they have any. Also, pay an attorney the $40 or $50 buck for a consultation. This is time well spent, especially do establish a repoire with your attorney. You can personalize yourself and establish a likeable relationship with your attorney.

About the Author

Brandon McClain is a practicing attorney who specializes in criminal defense, along with other legal specialties. McClain has experienced the United States judicial system from all vantage points from being a defendant to being a prosecutor.

Prison Planet

How to Avoid Becoming Another Statistic

Brandon McClain J.D.

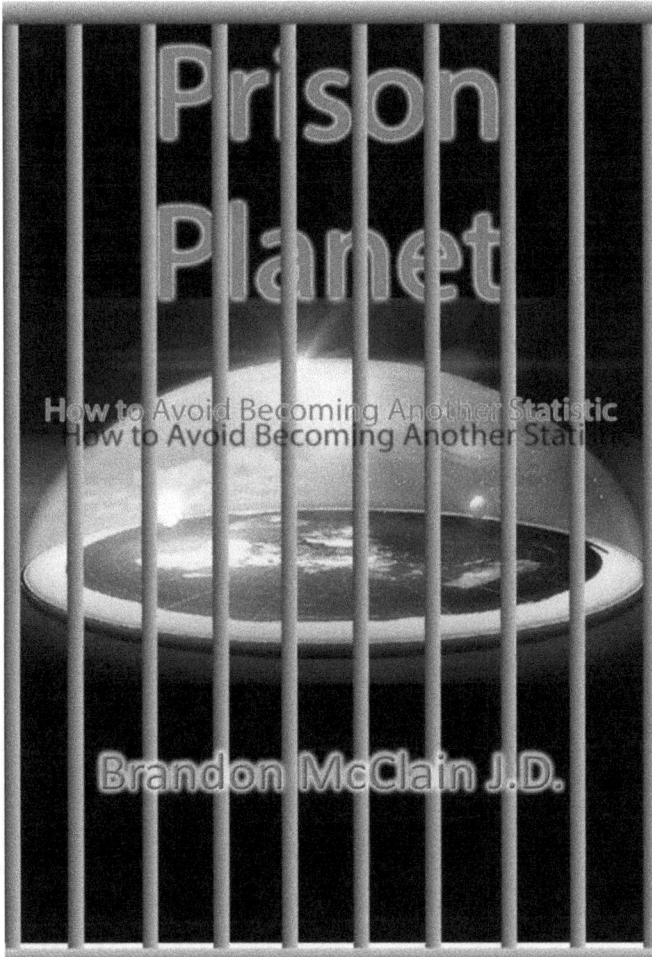

UP**TOWN**
MEDIA JOINT VENTURES
PUBLISHING

www.ingramcontent.com/pod-product-compliance
Lightning Source LLC
Chambersburg PA
CBHW060516210326
41520CB00015B/4230